T0067484

Queen's Spirit

Chatter in the Doorway

JAGN

authorHOUSE®

AuthorHouse™
1663 Liberty Drive
Bloomington, IN 47403
www.authorhouse.com
Phone: 1 (800) 839-8640

Published by AuthorHouse 08/13/2015

ISBN: 978-1-5049-3188-5 (sc)
ISBN: 978-1-5049-3189-2 (e)

Scripture quotations marked KJV are from the Holy Bible, King James Version (Authorized Version). First published in 1611. Quoted from the KJV Classic Reference Bible, Copyright © 1983 by The Zondervan Corporation.

Print information available on the last page.

Any people depicted in stock imagery provided by Thinkstock are models, and such images are being used for illustrative purposes only. Certain stock imagery © Thinkstock.

This book is printed on acid-free paper.

Proverbs 27:1 Boast not thyself of tomorrow; for thou knowest not what a day may bring forth.

Prayer

Lord, thank you for allowing your daughters to stop, to listen and to realize we are in a spiritual warfare. Forgive us Lord for the sins we have committed. We know it is time for us to take a spiritual inventory of our lives based on God's Word. We thank the Holy Spirit for revealing to us that we are not wrestling against flesh and blood but against principalities, against powers, against the rulers of the darkness of this world, against spiritual wickedness in high places. Lord, please help us not to be weak-willed women, loaded down with sin and swayed by all kind of evil desires. Give us enough wisdom to cancel every assignment, sever all soul ties and break every curse that has been loosed against your children. Lord, help us not to try and control people by witchcraft and charm. We close the doors now and seal the doorways with the blood of Jesus. Lord we have a desire to hide the word in our hearts so we may not sin against thee. Lord we thank you for your continuous guidance and insight in the name of Jesus. AMEN

Scriptures

Isaiah 22:22 And the key of the house of David will I lay upon his shoulder; so he shall open, and none shall shut; and he shall shut, and none shall open.

Matthew 16:19 And I will give unto thee the keys of the kingdom of heaven, and whatsoever thou shalt bind on earth shall be bound in heaven, and whatsoever thou shalt loose on earth shall be loosed in heaven.

Romans 8:15 For ye have not received the spirit of bondage again to fear; but ye have received the Spirit of adoption, whereby we cry, Abba, Father.

Romans 8:38-39 For I am persuaded, that neither death, nor life, nor angels, nor principalities, nor powers, nor things present, nor things to come, Nor height, nor depth, nor any other creature, shall be able to separate us from the love of God, which is in Christ Jesus our Lord.

Joshua 1:9 Have not I commanded thee? Be strong and of a good courage; be not afraid, neither be thou dismayed: for the Lord thy God is with thee whithersoever thou goest.

Psalm 36:11 Let not the foot of pride come against me, and let not the hand of the wicked remove me.

Proverbs 6:26 For by means of a whorish woman a man is brought to a piece of bread; and the adulteress will hunt for the precious life.

Proverbs 17:13 Whoso rewardeth evil for good, evil shall not depart from his house.

Proverbs 24:1 Be not thou envious against evil men, neither desire to be with them.

Proverbs 28:13 He that coverth his sins shall not prosper; but whoso confesseth and forsaketh them shall have mercy.

The New Open Bible: Study Edition
Copyright @1990 by Thomas Nelson Inc.

Dedication

God is the only holy, true and living God. It is God who has given me this opportunity through His son Jesus to write about this queen's spirit. I have nothing to offer but prayers, praises and thanksgiving. Bless His Holy name.

Introduction

Ladies, this book is for every woman whether young, old, seasoned or silly. There is a bold spirit riding through the land and it is trying to sift the people of God. This is a message for women who have this kind of spirit, know someone with this spirit, know someone fighting with this spirit, know someone without this spirit, know someone who is unaware of this spirit, know someone who crossed to the same side because of this spirit, know someone who wants to be free from this spirit or know someone placed in her path by the Lord. Wait!!! Please, before casting the first stone you must read and then you will be able to receive. I know you are probably thinking, oh she is talking about the spirit of Jezebel. Listen to me ladies, not this time; she is most wicked than Jezebel could have ever been. Your mind may be saying, there is no way, but I will share with you what the Bible says about this exceedingly wicked queen's spirit. The things this twisted spirit brings to the mind of people to say, think, or do is truly evil, selfish and against what the Bible teaches. This evil spirit will try and destroy or control everyone who gets in her path. Her wicked spirit has left a bitter memory mark with many women, men, boys and girls. Her approach is very subtle and veiled. I know her name, some of her enticements, and I want you to know. For now, we will refer to her as Queen's spirit but her real name is Athaliah. Remember, greater is he that is in you than he that is in the world. Please, I encourage you to pray, dress yourself in the armor of God, get your weapon (Ladies, the Bible) and prepare yourself for the reading of this book. Let us look for the doorway to her plot. I want you to know that she loves to evil chat.

Chapter 1

Moments of Reflection

I was sitting in my favorite chair, by the window, on a very rainy day in July. I could hear the rain beating against the window and it sounded like music to my ears. Rain restores the earth like the Holy Spirit refreshes my soul. I began to talk to the Holy Spirit about some of the joys and sorrows in my life. I was so thankful for all of the dangers and toils that He had delivered me in, preserved me from, and saved me in the midst of. Oh, how I could feel His present. I began thinking about all of the victories in my life and became overwhelmed by the goodness of God. Now as you know, this peace was too good, so truly it had to be interrupted. The telephone rang and I rose to answer it. It was a girlfriend calling to let me know that she had just filed for a divorce. I began to cry and yell, please do not let Satan win, do not let him win, you cannot let this happen. I told her God is not pleased with this. My friend began to tell me if she stays in her marriage, God will not be pleased with what she may do. I continued to talk and try to convince her to reconsider her decision. She asked me to pray for her and hung up. I was thinking; I regret receiving that phone call. I was feeling extremely sad in my heart, and I began to pray and ask God why there are so many attacks on marriages. I turned my face toward the window and began to weep bitterly. While I was weeping, a knock on the door resounded over the rain. I had been weeping so loud, that I hoped the person at the door did not hear me. Oh well, "go and answer the door girl," I said to myself. I answered the door and my God, I knew I was in for a long evening because my visitor and I are known to talk for hours without a coffee break. I knew we were going to enjoy the presence of the Holy Spirit, praise God, pray, worship and have Bible study, all in one night. The Holy Spirit said to me, I want you to listen to what this person is about to tell you. I braced myself, stopped my tears and invited the person in. We sat down, just to talk, and he said, "I need to tell you about a dream." He sat with a perplexed look on his face. I asked him to tell me about the dream, but I let him know that the Holy Spirit had not empowered me to interpret dreams. My visitor proceeded to share his story of a recurring dream that he had been having all through his life, until age seventeen. It was so frightening and real it had terrorized him. The dream was about a witch, with a hatchet in her hand, chasing him. Each time the witch would get close enough to take a swing, she would try to chop the legs from underneath him. This continued for years until he got married. The dream stopped but the evil spirit did not. My friend and his wife were so young when they married and did not fully understand spiritual warfare. Sadly, the marriage ended with a divorce. The spirit of the witch in those dreams began to work in ways not familiar to most of us. The Queen evil spirit's job is to bring a person down to disgrace. God's grace though will always raise us up and give us mercy for the journey.

My visitor told me he needed to be going and as he left I was pondering, Lord, what does this dream mean? The Holy Spirit told me to pick up my Bible and provided the scripture to turn to for my answer. I obeyed the Lord and was very surprised at the scripture I was reading. I began reading 2Kings, chapter 8. How many times do we read a passage in the Bible and not even think about it? Lord, I would not have known this unless the Holy Spirit revealed it to me. Then, I began reading, writing and studying about this Queen's controlling spirit. I said, "Lord, if you give me the strength I will pen what you want me to say to your daughters." They cry out day and night to be delivered from this tormenting spirit of this cursed woman. The brokenness and barrenness causes some of your daughters to surrender the battle too quickly. The pressure is great but our God is greater. Lord, your daughters truly want to be obedient, committed and set apart for your use. Your daughters want to keep their vows before and after marriage, they do not wish to bring shame to you. Sometimes the baggage someone else is carrying can be a distraction. The queen's luggage has a lot of compartments filled with fiery weapons.

Chapter 2

The Queen's Baggage

Her luggage is fully loaded with all kinds of destructive ammunition. She wants to destroy the anointing in the lives of God's children. She is well prepared for her game. Her conniving, controlling, manipulating and dominating spirit is unleashed in the land. She creates havoc among God's daughters on a daily basis. One of the areas she loves to divide is the covenant of marriage. She blocks the glory of God in marriage by sending her seducing spirits to bring ruin. Her target is to attack the man, because he is the head of the woman in marriage. She is supremely enticing and well-practiced in deception. Since I am talking first to married women, we will take a look at some of her seductive, deceptive and enticing characteristics. Let's take a look into her baggage before she shows her ticket for pickup. The evil one's enticement affects a marriage socially, financially, physically, sexually, emotionally and spiritually. These are just a few of her secret enticements that yield embarrassment to the women of God. Now, we will look into the six compartments of her luggage.

Socially

This is the area where self esteem and self worth is attacked and may lead many to hopelessness, depression, alienation and insomnia. This wicked Queen can entice a man to ask his wife to stay home, while he takes the mistress to public places. He does not allow his wife to spend time with friends or family, and leaves his wife in the middle of the night to meet other women. He will despise his wife and hate his own mother. He will take his wife on a vacation, but the mistress will be with him most of time. This evil enticer will have him go into the family home and change clothes while the mistress is waiting in the car. He denies his wife in the presence of a crowd. The man can tell this deceiver all about his wife, while she knows nothing about the mistress. He will refuse a full course meal with his wife to eat a $1 hamburger with his mistress.

Financially

This is the area where the necessities in life are funded with monies. If the funds are misused it causes strife, quarreling, fighting and frustration. She can entice a man in a marriage to abuse family finances by taking the family monies and giving it to his mistress, allowing another woman to drive his car while the wife is paying the note; take money from their family account to pay another woman's bills. He will buy gifts with family monies, take his check to another woman for her needs, allow other women to buy him things he likes with the wife's money, and he will permit the mistress to max out the wife's credit cards to fulfill her selfish desires. He takes money from their family account to pay child support for a child not conceived from his seed.

Physically

This is the area where some type of evidence, invisible or visible is left to prove a point. If the physical abuse is not dealt with it may generate anxiety, insanity, sickness, fear of men, resentment and death. She can entice a man to abuse the wife that loves him, beat his wife until no breath is left; beat his wife because the beans burnt. He will leave his wife and come to his mistress's rescue, leave evidence of his infidelity in view of his wife, disease his wife from infidelity and require the wife to pay for medication and doctor visits. Most of all, this queen spirit is known for boosting his ego by making him feel like he is the only man in the world with his qualities.

Sexually

This is the area where the pain is inward and it hurts the heart the most. This is least talked about and the weight becomes a burden for the heart. This kind of attack may produce self-pity, rejection, envy, distrust, self-seduction, adultery and fantasy lust.

She can entice a man to think of the mistress in the midst of time with his spouse, not to ever touch his wife again, seduce another woman in the presence of his wife. He will occupy their marriage bed with another woman, while his wife is at work. He will create a constant reminder of the infidelity by having children out of wedlock, and believe she is the only woman capable of pleasing him. He will get up out of a warm bed and embrace the cold, just to see her. Make movies of his affairs and watch them in his wife's presence, crawl out of the window at midnight to go watch pornography. He may stay out all night long and not know why, be harsh in the special private chambers of the wife's life, request actions that grip your very soul, perform disgusting acts with young girls and impregnate other women and tell his wife, I did this for you.

Emotionally

This is the area where the evil one attacks the most and it is all in the mind. If your mind is under attack it becomes difficult to think spiritually and the evil one knows it.

She can entice a man and encrypt his mind to think and see just her; he changes his wardrobe, walk and talk, and lies about a simple phone call. He goes to see the mistress even while the wife begs him to stay home. He will burn rubber vehicle tires in the wife's face to get to his mistress. He will dial the wife's number and give the mistress the phone to tell his wife his location, call his wife another woman's name and laugh. He will miss the birth of his first child. He is so nice to his wife that she never expects another woman in the picture. He stops gambling and brings his mistress his entire check. He believes his behavior is correct and makes meeting arrangements with his lover while the wife is waiting on the other line. He becomes so comfortable being controlled by her, believes he is the best and she cannot live without him, will take food from his house to her house. Sometimes a man will smoke crack and this queen spirit may control him for a lifetime. He will brave a storm to meet her at another man's house, believe whatever she says without question. He writes another woman's name on his wife's birthday card. He forgets his wife's birthday. He picks the mistress up, in his wife's car, while the wife is waiting at the bus stop in the rain. He will go from one woman to another all in the same day. He will leave his job at lunch and never return. This wicked queen will entice him to leave everything he owns and follow her destructive pathway to ruin.

Spiritually

This queen's vindictive spirit wants to be worshiped. Her role is to entice and rob the men of God of every spiritual blessing reducing them to spiritual paupers. The Bible says in Ephesians 5:22-23, 29-33.

22 Wives, submit yourselves unto your own husbands, as unto the Lord.
23 For the husband is the head of the wife, even as Christ is the head of the church: and he is the saviour of the body.

²⁹ For no man ever yet hated his own flesh; but nourisheth and cherisheth it, even as the Lord the church:
³⁰ For we are members of his body, of his flesh, and of his bones.
³¹ For this cause shall a man leave his father and mother, and shall be joined unto his wife, and they two shall be one flesh.
³² This is a great mystery: but I speak concerning Christ and the church.
³³ Nevertheless let every one of you in particular so love his wife even as himself; and the wife see that she reverence her husband.

Now, the understanding is becoming partially clear why enticing men of God is so important to the wicked one. She may know how to nourish his flesh but will destroy his soul. Queen believes if the head is destroyed, the plan of God will not prevail. God is in marriages that have and will survive her attacks. Her motive is to shift men living holy lives to a life as womanizing whores. She can convince men she is listening but destroy them with their own words. Her evil spirit goes to any length to seek who she can devour. Her main goal is to hinder the Word of God by attacking the men of God. She manipulates them by quoting passages from the Bible or prophesying a lie about what God has spoken. Men receive warnings from spouses but spouses are manipulated to believe their instincts are from the devil. In most occasions, the decline of the man's faith is progressively clear. The man is gradually drawn away from his relationship with God. He ignores God's voice and thinks prayer is no longer needed. His false belief grows that God will bless this kind of behavior. He is blinded to the valley of destruction approaching. The queen's goal is to destroy men of God and interfere with men that want to become children of God. Athaliah killed members of her own family, what do you think she will do to you? Listen, do not be fooled, there are men who can resist her enticements, regardless of the measures she goes through. God has some real men soldiers in his army. Sometimes the man can detect the spirit of Athaliah and inform his wife to guard against her. Wives, this is the time to use our God given weapons and close the doorway to her plot. Remember, she loves to chat at the doorway.

Ladies, let me pause here for a second and ask if you see any resemblance of her in your life? Shall I continue? There is much more, but I seek not to glorify this deceptive Queen's spirit. I wish to expose her. She may have impressive ways. If we continue to glorify her we may help open the very doorway we are trying to close. Did you get comfortable and let her in the doorway? Ladies, is she in your relationship? If she is, start the spiritual battle to get her out quickly. If she is not, guard yourselves against her deceptions. Do not listen to the Queen's chat.

Chapter 3

If You Had Known

So, what are you to do if you are the woman fighting this deceptive Queen's spirit? This woman is a woman of war and is hurting because she is fighting against flesh and blood. A scorned woman births revenge, hatred and evil in her heart. She lacks the knowledge of this evil spirit's plans. The often used quote is, "I will pay you back if it is the last thing I do in this life". Every day the scorned woman arises filled with a vengeful spirit. She will look for others to help her plot revenge and will seek ungodly advice. This hurting woman needs knowledge of spiritual warfare and only the Holy Ghost can teach her this warfare. Her pain is so intense and consuming that the only person she thinks about is herself. The question is always, am I that weak? How long can this continue? This scorned woman can become territorial, bold and arrogant. She begins to resemble the nature of the evil spirit she is fighting. (Remember the old saying, if you can't beat them, join them). Daughter it is nothing you have done, it is what you are not doing. We as women are always learning but rarely share our weaknesses and faults. I know you are wondering, then, how can she be stopped. Perhaps you have cried, pleaded by the blood of Jesus, prayed, fasted, read scriptures and nothing seems to happen. All those weapons you use slow her down and even stop her for a while. The Holy Spirit, our comforter, says I will uproot this evil spirit and you will see her no more. Everything associated with her will be buried but not within you.

Ladies, how many of you has she enslaved in a cave of darkness, working her power of ruin through your spouse? This can manifest as depression, suicidal or homicidal thoughts. Jezebel caused Elijah to run from her into a cave. This queen's evil spirit is most wicked than Jezebel. Look, she causes men to build their own caves and hide in them. Men are building getaways and glorying in it. They do not understand that if they are not being led by the Holy Spirit, trouble is waiting at the door called divorce. Ladies, you have been fighting with him for so long and believing it is your new normal. Just as you make up your mind to leave, Athaliah will release her stronghold for a moment. He will act like he is willing to do the righteous thing, for a while. God's daughters increase their hope, and this wicked queen thinks that you have been fooled again. Ladies, you think if I had only known. I say, in your knowledge, bring war against this wicked spirit. Stop playing with the door knob and get away from the doorway.

Chapter 4

Get Something Out of This

Now, there may be ladies that will never have to deal with this spirit. Perhaps, their parents prayed for them diligently, even before they were conceived. Please be grateful she missed your house, because the curse is broken. The bible says in Jeremiah 29:11, For I know the thoughts that I think toward you, saith the Lord, thoughts of peace, and not of evil, to give you an expected end. Maybe this was not in God's divine will for your life. If she does not attack you in marriage or any affiliation with marriage, she will look for other avenues to work her plan. Do not laugh when you see her attacks working in the lives of other. She has a spirit that wants to kill, steal and destroy. Now, since you will never have to deal with this spirit in an antagonizing manner, let us thank God for his power and love. Daughters like you are needed in the body of Christ for intercessions and powerful warfare. A Proverbs 31 woman means absolutely nothing to the evil one but everything to God. The Proverbs 31 woman is a wife of noble character, worth more than the price of rubies, her husband has full confidence in her, she brings him good all the days of her life, she works with eager hands, she considers a field and buys it, she uses her earnings wisely, she open her arms to the poor, extends her hands to the needy, she speaks with wisdom, faithful instruction is on her tongue, she watches over the affairs of her household and does not eat the bread of idleness. God's daughters are secure because of the power of God. That seductive spirit is Satan's best but we are God's best. I must commend the women who married men with the spirit of Joseph. How well you must sleep at night and elevate your head in the midst of her heist. Women like you will still be able to get something out of this. Other women, maybe you need to appreciate and recognize the God fearing man you have been blessed with. It will make you pray for yourself as well as others. It will make you alert and oriented for the journey. The main thing you will be able to do is truly worship and praise God for His goodness and mercy. Women like you are able to close the door, cover it, seal it, and hold the keys in your hand, by the power of the blood of Jesus.

Chapter 5

Her Surprise Visit

Ladies, there are some of you who never knew about this spirit. All along as women, we thought the spirit of Jezebel was the worst spirit on land, in the air or by water. I never knew this wicked spirit, but I certainly heard about many of her attributes. I know some of you really do not know this deceptive spirit. Guess what, I did not know until the Holy Spirit removed the blinders from my eyes. Queen's wicked spirit will call you Ms. Denial, but daughters walk with me, and help expose this conniving one. If you have not had an encounter with her, I promise you have heard about her enticing ways working in the lives of others. Now, think what you said when you heard about her secret enticements of your best friend's spouse. Speak truth. Did you tell her not to put up with that, to move to another relationship, to stay in it and make it as terrible as possible for him, to try and make it work, get you somebody as well, go on with your life, you are not getting any younger, or that two can play that game. Did you think to tell her to seek the Holy Ghost? Single ladies please stay with Jesus and He will send you whom he deems fit for your life. I know what some of you are saying, I'm tired of waiting, my clock is winding down, what does she know, it will not happen to me, I got this. Singles ladies controlled and manipulated by this evil spirit, are you thinking, I will not get caught, the money is good, and he said he was going to leave his wife for me. Ladies, that kind of talk is chatter. Remember, it is coming up again and you may be the recipient. Ok, you have been waiting for a long time for your Boaz. Every time a man passes by or someone introduces you to a friend, are you wondering Lord is this the one? God decides it is time for the arrival of Mr. Allofthat. Are we happy or what? He finds you and the two of you become one. This is just what you wanted until what you used to be, becomes active in your marriage by someone else. You failed to pay attention and did not repent. A surprise visit by the queen's evil spirit is how she will set you up. She loves to destroy marriages, dreams and careers. The godly seasonal women tried to warn you for what lie ahead. Do not stumble and live below the poverty line. If you take on this queen's spirit evil lies at the door. You are beloved by God. God has a great plan for your life. The single ladies that decide to wait, all I can say is, no one can tell your story like you can. Oh my God help us to close this door so our children and loved ones can be relieved from this burden and pain. Ladies, your home is a place of comfort, not chaos. Women please stop speaking the phrase, "that is just how men are and will be." Stop it, life and death are in the power of our tongues. We speak life into our situation and the lives of others. We will from this day and moving forward, confess, Jesus Christ is my Lord and this will not continue on my watch. Stop her because she has already made enough surprise visits. Please do not trust in yourself and open the door to her. Trust in the Lord. Say, I am a watchman on the wall and I will be watchful and mindful of what is permitted in my life in the name of Jesus.

Chapter 6

I am Held by Her Grip

I am talking to the women who have crossed over to the same side because of this wicked and controlling spirit. Yes, I am talking to the lesbians. God loves you and so do the women of God. We need you all to help expose and tear down this destroying spirit that is riding through the land. This evil spirit is leaving a tornado effect in the lives of God's people. I do not know why you crossed over, but I know how you can get back. Jesus is the way and is waiting on you to ask him for your deliverance. Some women have gotten into that state of mind because of the hurt left by a damaging relationship with a male and so many other reasons. Ladies do not give up because there are still some Spirit led men in the world. If at all possible, learn to love yourself. There is nothing wrong with living a righteous life. Please ask yourself, why do I want to imitate someone who has hurt me, become someone I can never be or allow my imagination to run away with me? The Queen's wicked spirit really wants to hold on to the all of you. You may be feeling you are held by her grip and cannot get loose. This is how she desires you to feel. She will invite the Succubus or Incubus spirit to come into your life. These are the sexual demons that enjoy making appearances in your dreams. She knows the lesbian, when repentance occurs, will be a terror to her in the body of Christ. The body of Christ needs you. God is calling for the ones that have left their first love, never felt love, do not know how to love, are looking for love, and are ready to be loved and to learn that God is love. The Bible says, For God so loved the world, that he gave his only begotten Son, that whosoever believeth in him should not perish, but have everlasting life. For God sent not his Son into the world to condemn the world; but that the world through him might be saved. John 3:16-17(New Open Bible). You have entered the doorway to her plot but the door is still open. I know all you can hear is chatter, chatter and chatter. Stop it.

Chapter 7

I Know Your Next Move

We may know someone or you may be the person, living under the influence of this spirit and want to be free of her. We may know it is an attack from the forces of darkness but cannot understand why the chains remain unbroken. The biblical principles that have been learned and taught have been applied in our daily lives. We have prayed, fasted, cried, mourned, rolled over on the floor or ground, spent the night at a conference, listened to every gospel sermon, looked for someone believing to get a prayer to God, stood in every prayer line, read every scripture possible, wanted a word from every true prophet, eagerly arrived at the house of God and the list goes on and on. Many may think that it is like God is not coming to your rescue. Most women may think that this is a bad spirit, but we serve the only true, great, and living God. Do not give up. Help is already here. She will be stopped. It is amazing that we as daughters of God, in a crisis or under attack, often forget about our past victories when God revealed himself in a divine and magnificent way.

Being a God fearing woman, holy and set apart unto God, does matter to Him. What she once did, no more says the Lord. She may have made some throw in the towel, throw up their hands, and throw away dreams. She may be a dream killer to some but God makes us dream keepers. I am looking for ladies to encourage and travel with me through this valley. I promise you the weapons you are using work. Smile, you will come out victorious. Remember, we are already victorious because of what Christ did on the cross. Jesus extended his love eternally, by being raised from the dead by his Father, and now sits on the right hand of his Father, interceding for us. We know Christ will never leave us alone and that is why He sent the Holy Spirit. We must remember He did this just for us and makes it personal, because it is. Do not give up because your deliverance is too close. God heard the groans and knows the pain you are enduring. Please do not except her wicked spirit through the man in your life. Do not take her conniving spirit into your bosom because it is too close to your heart. I want to speak life and hope to you. When you are free, you will see the king in him instead of that treacherous spirit. You have the vision and the tools; watch God work through you and the queen's wicked spirit will know it is God. She will not see this coming. God is such a good God. It will be healthy for you, regardless of how God chooses to free you. Remember, that you will continue in relationship with God and that is how it should be. Declare to yourself, I will draw nearer to God and He will draw nigh to me. Ladies, let me hear you say, because of the Holy Ghost, I know your next move Queen. We close the door to your plot. I can't listen to the chatter in the doorway anymore.

Chapter 8

Out of this Wreck I Rise

Some women have been placed in her path by the Lord. The Holy God has chosen you for such a time as this. You can stand the test to bring a revolution against this dominating spirit, with all the power of the kingdom of God. She is unaware it is time for her to be thrust out of the window of your life. All along ladies you have been in training for reigning. You may feel like Paul and his men at the shipwreck. Remember, some swam in the waters, some held on boards, some on broken pieces but all made it to land safely. All of us can be used by God but are delivered differently. It is not what you go through but know who you belong to. If you know who you belong to, it does not matter what you go through. When you have been placed in her path by God, many questions are asked and comments are made at first. Lord, did you really place me here? How long will I be here, because it is a terrible place to be? I do not deserve this. If this is really from God, pray that you are a willing vessel. Is God really in the midst of this? God do you really love me? This is a place where flesh is to die daily. It hurts so bad because the Lord will not get you out until He decides it is time. Not knowing what God is doing makes a person want to give up. Then, you realize if you give up, where will you go or who would you turn to? The only answer is to the Lord, to the Lord. The Holy Ghost is the only one who can give you peace. Once you have the assurance of the Holy Spirit, then it becomes a joy to be persecuted. Then, you will say with boldness, if I perish let me perish because I have been sent by the King for this assignment. I have put my hand to the plow and will not turn back. These are the ladies brought in for the cause of Christ. They will say, God has this and enjoy the ride. A barrier has been turned into a bridge that will carry you into your next season. Now, you can bless others because of what God has given to you. The more grateful you are, the more you give. Then, you will understand and live according to the rules of Kingdom Life coming from Luke 6:27-38.

27	But I say unto you which hear, Love your enemies, do good to them which hate you,
28	Bless them that curse you, and pray for them which despitefully use you.
29	And unto him that smiteth thee on the one cheek offer also the other; and him that taketh away thy cloak forbid not to take thy coat also.
30	Give to every man that asketh of thee; and of him that taketh away thy goods ask them not again.
31	And as ye would that men should do to you, do ye also to them likewise.

32	For if ye love them which love you, what thank have ye? for sinners also love those that love them.
33	And if ye do good to them which do good to you, what thank have ye? for sinners also do even the same.
34	And if ye lend to them of whom ye hope to receive, what thank have ye? for sinners also lend to sinners, to receive as much again.
35	But love ye your enemies, and do good, and lend, hoping for nothing again; and your reward shall be great, and ye shall be the children of the Highest: for he is kind unto the unthankful and to the evil.
36	Be ye therefore merciful, as your Father also is merciful.
37	Judge not, and ye shall not be judged: condemn not, and ye shall not be condemned: forgive, and ye shall be forgiven:
38	Give, and it shall be given unto you; good measure, pressed down, and shaken together, and running over, shall men give into your bosom. For with the same measure that ye mete withal it shall be measured to you again.

You know because of the indwelling of the Godhead, you will not be defeated. God gave us hope when we had no hope and could not see His way. The Holy Ghost will let you know that this enemy (Queen's spirit) you will see no more. The women of God will continue to praise and worship God for what He has done. This doorway is finally closed. Because of the awesome power of the Holy Ghost we can declare, out of this wreck I rise.

Chapter 9

No More Chatter From The Queen

Yes, ladies I know you have been waiting and wondering, who is this wicked and notorious Queen's spirit? Again, I tell you it is Queen Athaliah. The hidden message is that she is the one that has created and caused so much havoc in our lives and others. Her shameful attacks are to destroy men and affect the lives of God's daughters. It's time for us to stop using her enticing tactics and repeating her chatter. Ladies, I am listening. Speak!!!! She played a role in my marriage causing it to fail. She played a role in draining the family finances. She provoked me to dislike men. She enticed me with fear of marriage. She provoked me to target only married men. She enticed me to think that God was punishing me. She made me believe that a good marriage would never happen for me. She enticed me to believe I did not need a man. She enticed me to change men like outfits. She enticed me to except any type of relationship. She enticed me to target spiritual leaders for sex.

Stop the chatter and get your hope back. We must build on our most holy faith.

The Holy Ghost has opened our eyes so we do not have to deal with her directly anymore. We must begin to thank God for positioning us for such a time as this. Jesus has the power to keep us from her sting. If this is our path, He can protect and keep us. No more chatter from the Queen. Well, it is time to call her out. She has been hiding too long. She has been covered too long by Jezebel's spirit. This is the last time we will call her Queen's spirit and refer to her real name which is Athaliah. God has unveiled her to his daughters through His word. You can come forth now, "Queen Athaliah".

Chapter 10

Bible based facts about
Queen Athaliah

Athaliah (means whom Jehovah has afflicted) was the only ruling queen of both Judah and Israel. She was the granddaughter of Omri and the daughter of King Ahab and Queen Jezebel of Israel. She married the king of Judah (Jehoram) which was a part of Satan's design so idolatry could be introduced in the area of Judah. Mother like daughter, Athaliah was to do to Judah the same as what Jezebel did to Israel. It was Satan's plan to enter into the royal line seeking to stop and destroy the possibility of the Seed of the woman coming into the world. Jehoram reigned for eight years and did that which was evil in the eyes of the Lord. Jehoram, Athaliah's husband, killed his six brethren with the sword. In a raid on Jehoram's house by the Philistines, Arabs and Ethiopians, property was looted and all of Jehoram's sons were killed, except for the youngest one. Jehoram died of an incurable disease. Ahaziah was made king after the death of his father. His mother was his counselor in giving instructions to do evil. After one year of reigning as king, Ahaziah was killed by Jehu whom the Lord anointed to cut off the house of Ahab. When Athaliah, mother of Ahaziah found out he was dead, she arose and destroyed all the seed royal of the house of Judah. Now, look at what Athaliah did. She killed her grandchildren and other close relatives to *increase* her political control. Look at God, Joash was the only one left in the line of the coming Messiah. Joash was hid for six years and Athaliah reigned for six years. Davidic covenant promised a king on the throne of Judah as long as they had a kingdom with any potentials of righteousness. Jehoiada the high priest plotted the overthrow of Athaliah to restore the rightful heir to the throne of Judah and bring back the worship of Jehovah again. He needed some help so he called all of the rulers of the guards to the temple and made a covenant with them. He made an oath with them and showed them the king's son. He wanted them to agree with him to protect the king's son, take part in the rebellion, and overthrow Athaliah. Now, they were brave enough to bring the king's son out of the temple, crown him, anoint him, and gave him a copy of the Law of Moses. The Law of Moses allowed Joash to be able to govern and mete out justice to the people. Guess what, Athaliah did not know anything of this nature was happening. These people were plotting her death and she did not know it. The heart breaker, she thought she had killed all the heirs to the throne and was safe. How did she miss this? Be careful, you do not know what a day may bring. Ok, let's read the bible based facts.

Please turn with me to 2 Kings 11:1-21 in the KJV and you will find these scripture written:

11:1	And when Athaliah the mother of Ahaziah saw that her son was dead, she arose and destroyed all the seed royal.
11:2	But Jehosheba, the daughter of king Joram, sister of Ahaziah, took Joash the son of Ahaziah, and stole him from among the king's sons which were slain; and they hid him, even him and his nurse, in the bedchamber from Athaliah, so that he was not slain.
11:3	And he was with her hid in the house of the LORD six years. And Athaliah did reign over the land.
11:4	And the seventh year Jehoiada sent and fetched the rulers over hundreds, with the captains and the guard, and brought them to him into the house of the LORD, and made a covenant with them, and took an oath of them in the house of the LORD, and showed them the king's son.
11:5	And he commanded them, saying, This is the thing that ye shall do; A third part of you that enter in on the sabbath shall even be keepers of the watch of the king's house;
11:6	And a third part shall be at the gate of Sur; and a third part at the gate behind the guard: so shall ye keep the watch of the house, that it be not broken down.
11:7	And two parts of all you that go forth on the sabbath, even they shall keep the watch of the house of the LORD about the king.
11:8	And ye shall compass the king round about, every man with his weapons in his hand: and he that cometh within the ranges, let him be slain: and be ye with the king as he goeth out and as he cometh in.

11:9	And the captains over the hundreds did according to all things that Jehoiada the priest commanded: and they took every man his men that were to come in on the sabbath, with them that should go out on the sabbath, and came to Jehoiada the priest.
11:10	And to the captains over hundreds did the priest give king David's spears and shields, that were in the temple of the LORD.
11:11	And the guard stood, every man with his weapons in his hand, round about the king, from the right corner of the temple to the left corner of the temple, along by the altar and the temple.
11:12	And he brought forth the king's son, and put the crown upon him, and gave him the testimony; and they made him king, and anointed him; and they clapped their hands, and said, God save the king.
11:13	And when Athaliah heard the noise of the guard and of the people, she came to the people into the temple of the LORD.
11:14	And when she looked, behold, the king stood by a pillar, as the manner was, and the princes and the trumpeters by the king, and all the people of the land rejoiced, and blew with trumpets: and Athaliah rent her clothes, and cried, Treason, Treason.
11:15	But Jehoiada the priest commanded the captains of the hundreds, the officers of the host, and said unto them, Have her forth without the ranges: and him that followeth her kill with the sword. For the priest had said, Let her not be slain in the house of the LORD.

11:16	And they laid hands on her; and she went by the way by the which the horses came into the king's house: and there was she slain.
11:17	And Jehoiada made a covenant between the LORD and the king and the people, that they should be the LORD's people; between the king also and the people.
11:18	And all the people of the land went into the house of Baal, and brake it down; his altars and his images brake they in pieces thoroughly, and slew Mattan the priest of Baal before the altars. And the priest appointed officers over the house of the LORD.
11:19	And he took the rulers over hundreds, and the captains, and the guard, and all the people of the land; and they brought down the king from the house of the LORD, and came by the way of the gate of the guard to the king's house. And he sat on the throne of the kings.
11:20	And all the people of the land rejoiced, and the city was in quiet: and they slew Athaliah with the sword beside the king's house.
11:21	Seven years old was Jehoash when he began to reign.

Also, for additional reading go to 2 Chronicles: 22 - 23.

Chapter 11

She Has Been Defeated

Oh, the mind games that Athaliah's spirit plays, but she has been conquered. Ladies, stop talking so much about the problems she is causing and start talking to the problem solver. The weapons of our warfare are not carnal but mighty through the obliteration of strongholds. Athaliah's defeat is displayed in your life when you challenge her by doing what God requires. Remember while she plays, you pray. Her wicked spirit may be manipulating him, but you are a part of him. While she works, you worship God. While she flirts, you fast. While she lies, you will continue to love. While she is stroking him, your love is strengthening him. While she teases him, you teach him by your lifestyle. While she baits him, you believe God holds fast to him. She has been tricking him, but you have been trusting in him. She thought it was turmoil, but you knew it was a test from God. She thought it was mistaken evil, but you took it for a motive to do something good. She thought it was pressure and it was, but now you persevere. She wanted you to see only the storm, but you stood still to see the salvation of the Lord. She wanted you to continue to live with this heartache, but you stayed in the hand of God. She wanted to make you fear, but you decided to renew your fellowship with the Almighty. She is Satan's best, but you are going to finally put her to rest. Your weapons (repentance, prayer, worshipping, fasting, meditating, praising, the Word, the blood of Jesus, your testimony, witnessing, being silent) do not change but how and when we use the weapons do. When we submit to God, then the devil will flee from you. What God has blessed cannot be cursed, and God will not reverse it. Athaliah had a well painted rainbow until her true colors were exposed by the Son. The spirit of enticement through her attacks of trickery was her doorway. She was dressed in her chatty armor ready to defeat. Her plot was to steal, kill and destroy the lives of the daughters of God. She knows something we may have forgotten and that is the power and authority God's daughters possess. Daughter you are equipped to stop her secret enticements, close the doorway to her plot and stop listening to her evil chat. Believe in what Jesus Christ has already done. He defeated her well over two thousand years ago on the cross at Calvary. Jesus went to hell and took the keys to hell and death. He rose from the grave with all power, being all power and has eternal power. Now, open the doorway into the presence of God.

Chapter 12

Jesus is The Door and The Way

Jesus is the door and the only way. Jesus said, I am the door: by me if any man enter in, he shall be saved, and shall go in and out, and find pasture. Jesus saith unto him, I am the way, the truth, and the life: no man cometh unto the Father, but by me. He can keep us from becoming chatters. He can set a watch before our mouths and keep the door of our lips. Thank God for Jesus and the working power of the Holy Spirit.

Daughters the chatter has stopped and the doorway to Athaliah's plot has been *closed*. All other routes *denied*. All assignments *cancelled* because of the BLOOD of JESUS.

Chapter 13

Ladies are you ready for a spiritual checkup?

- Have I admitted I may have this wicked spirit and need help? *Y / N*
- Are you on Facebook more than in the Bible book? *Y / N*
- Are you going to play the payback game or pray? *Y/ N*
- Can you finish the assignment in order to be a blessing to someone else? *Y / N*
- Are you too ashamed to share your testimony? *Y / N*
- Do you believe joy will ring from your soul again? *Y / N*
- Are you able to forgive during and after the battle? *Y / N*
- Do you feel that you are the only one attacking or under the attack? *Y / N*

- Are you taking too long to allow God to heal you? *Y / N*
- Are you allowing the Holy Spirit to guide you? *Y / N*
- What have you learned about you?
- What have you learned about others?
- What have you learned about Queen Athaliah's spirit?
- What have you learned about the Holy Spirit?

Look ladies; there is a path that leads to blessedness. You are now walking that path. Keep seeking the Holy Ghost.

OR

Look ladies, remember you reap what you sow, so be careful about the seeds you plant because they will surely grow.

Chapter 14

Notes of encouragement:

God is your strength, strong tower and cornerstone. God will help in times of trouble.

God was, God is and God always will be.

There may be a delay in the storm but deliverance will surely come.

God's grace is enough to carry us through the impossible.

The yoke of bondage can be broken by the power of God.

I will outlive what I have been through.

There is a way that seemeth right to a man but the end is death.

Heart Search:

- *Am I in denial that Queen Athalia's spirit may be influencing me?*
- *Did this destructive spirit ruin my relationship?*
- *Am I too ashamed to admit that I have been influenced and my mind poisoned by Athaliah's venom?*
- *Do I have the spirit of Athaliah?*
- *Am I so much like Athaliah, I can't see the difference?*
- *Will I ever trust again after living through such devastation?*
- *Am I angry with God for allowing the enemy to attack me?*
- *How can I inform women, who are blind to Athaliah's spirit?*
- *Do I know what actions are required to wage spiritual warfare against Athaliah's spirit?*
- *Now, am I bitter or better?*

Acknowledgment:

Very Special Thanks: Deacon James Ramon Nelson (Husband)

Churches: Men of God that watch out for my soul.

Greater Law Memorial Church of God in Christ Bishop Willie A. Jenkins Sr.

Greater Jerusalem Missionary Baptist Church Pastor Joe Fred Russell

Special Thanks:

Eddie Ruth Goodwin (mother)
Gloria Goodwin (cousin)
Vern Washington (friend)
Louis and Brenda Jackson (friends)
Monchez DA'Loushard Jackson (godson)
Aaden Trent Lewis (godson)
Lee Esther Protho (encourager)
A. Moody (editor)
Family, friends and coworkers

I can never forget the saints of God in the present or the past.

Published:
Topics For The Ages: Flowing Like A River
Just Like God To Whisper: Sweet Whispers
Mama's Pea Talk: What Says The Pea?

Printed in the United States
By Bookmasters